AF566721

AUGURY TODAY
A New Interpretation from Treya Meynack of Trevena & Philippa Agrippa of The Temple Mount

Based upon-
'Ornithomancy and Augury: An Illustrated Practical History'
by Master Occul of Lugdunum

Created by
Maria Kay Anthony

Dedication

This book is dedicated with love and gratitude to Master Skell, the former Chief Archivist of the Royal Trevena Kovskrifva: our friend, benefactor, and hero. *Philippa and Treya, 414 AD*

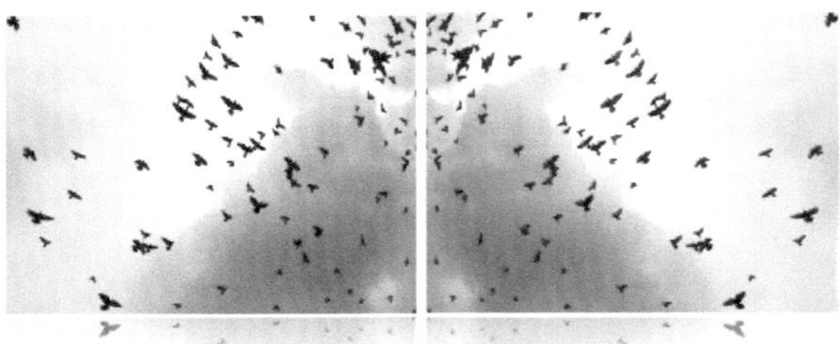

A note from the creator-

Philippa Agrippa and Treya Meynack are characters from my three-volume historical fantasy novel:

An Tir Gallósek, The Mighty Land

Pippa Agrippa in Britannia Prima
Marcus Constantinides in Albion Sub Terra
Treya Meynack in the Western Air

During their adventures, they became interested in augury, as did I. That led to the manifestation of Praefectus Augures Occul of Lugdunum and his text, which then inspired further study, from the characters, and from myself.

'Augury Today' is an original 'new' interpretation. The chronological ambiguity of the title reflects the fact that for thousands of years, people have been asking the same questions about life, destiny, and fate, and looking to the skies for answers.

Some information and quotes come from classical works, as noted throughout. The main reference books were 'Celtic Sacred Landscapes' by Nigel Pennick, 'A History of Pagan Europe' by Nigel Pennick and Prudence Jones, 'Rome' by M. Rostovtzeff, 'The Etruscans' by Graeme Baker and Tom Rasmussen, 'The White Goddess' by Robert Graves, and 'The Secret Teachings of All Ages' by Manly Hall. Images are either original, used by kind permission, or belong to the common treasuries of Wikipedia and Pixabay. Visual alchemy was created using Adobe Photoshop.

Maria Anthony

Borlowan
Books

Borlowan Books - POB 1554 - Lawrence, Kansas
USA 66044
borlowanbooks@gmail.com
@borlowanbooks
ISBN: 979-8-9920376-6-1

AUGURY
TODAY
A
NEW
INTERPRETATION

ABOUT THE AUGURS

Occulus Prefectus Augeres was the head of the Lugdunum Collage of Augury in Gaul, and the author of 'Ornithomancy and Augury: An Illustrated Practical History'. Master Occul had over fifty years of experience as a practitioner and a teacher. It was his life's goal to share the science of augury with others. He placed great emphasis on the sublime and divinely-connected experience of practicing ornithomancy, and much less on observing rigidly controlled rituals.

"The history of augury is an unbroken tradition of continual re-creation."
Occul of Lugdunum 11AD

Philippa Agrippa has been actively studying augury for ten years, but her connection to it goes back much further. When she was young, an augur predicted that she would achieve great things. As the only female Roman soldier in Britannia Prima, and a centurion at sixteen, she fulfilled the prophesy. She and Treya have travelled throughout the Britannic Isles and far beyond, from frozen Thule in the north, to Mauretania Tingitana in the south, and all the way east to Scythia and Sarmatia.
Philippa lives in Trevena, Kernow, with her husband and son, where she writes, teaches, and watches birds. She also enjoys sketching and painting them.

Treya Meynack has also been actively studying augury for ten years, but her interest in watching birds goes back to her childhood. She enjoys travelling to new places and she especially enjoys meeting new bird species, and the people who are interested in them. Treya is a professional scribe, and she has published several travel journals and maps, some specifically focused on bird migrations.
Treya lives with her husband and twin daughters in Trevena, Kernow, where she is the Chief Archivist of the Kovskrifva, the Royal Library. She is also, along with Philippa, a Royal Counsellor of the Court.

Preface-

After watching the birds together for the past ten years, we wanted to share our thoughts with anyone who might be interested in ornithomancy.

There are very few historical sources for augury available to us, so we relied mostly upon Master Occul's codex, as well as our own documented experiences.

Under each topic, we have provided the pertinent texts from Master Occul, after which we have added our own thoughts, when we've had them.

We are not experts, just dedicated scholar/practitioners. Our approach is eclectic, informal, and personalised. We respect and admire the Roman practices, and it is an honour to witness a traditional Roman Augur in action. But the story of augury didn't begin with Rome, nor will it end there. The history of bird divination is the history of humanity, encompassing thousands of years of widely diverse cultural practices, observations, and rituals.

We both have a deep appreciation for the art and science of ornithomancy, and we hope that this book will inspire the same in others.

Treya Meynack and Philippa Agrippa, Trevena, 414 AD

Contents:

The Introduction to the Original Text of 'Ornithomancy and Augury: An Illustrated Practical History'---

Occulus Praefectus Augures is the head of the Lugdunum College of Augury in Gallia Lugdunensis. He is the author of 'Ornithomancy and Augury: An Illustrated Practical History', as well as several published articles on the subject.

Master Occul has over fifty year of experience as a practitioner and a teacher. It is his life's goal to share the science of augury with others. He places great emphasis on the subliminal and personally divine experience of the practice, and far less on observing rigidly-controlled rituals.

"The history of augury is an unbroken tradition of continual re-creation."
Occul of Lugdunum, 11 AD

Our thoughts:

Lugdunum is a major city in Gaul, and it was the provincial Roman capitol of the province. It was (and still is) an important economic and administrative centre, so Occul and his associates would have been involved in official government actions, especially those of a military and judicial nature. They would have also served the general populace: individuals, couples, families, and businesses.

Philippa

The name Lugdunum means "hill or fortress of the god Lugus." Another Fortress of Lugh! The more I discover about Gaul, the more it reminds me of home.

Treya

Part One- Basic Ornithomancy

1. Augury and inauguration- auspicious and inauspicious omens

Augury is founded on the belief that birds, as creatures of the sky, can provide insights into the will of the gods, as well as predict the future. Augurs observe and record the direction of flight, the types of birds, the sounds they make, and whether they fly in groups or alone. Weather conditions are also taken into account. The augurs employ their observational skills to understand signs concerning divine pleasure or displeasure. These signs are called omens. When the practitioner, or augur, reads the signs, it is referred to as "taking the auspices".

The Greeks called it ornithomancy, from ορνις (ornis, fowl) and μαντεία (manteia, divination). Pliny the Elder traces bird augury to the prophet Tiresias, in ancient Thebes, sometime around 3200 BC. The Etruscans, Chaldeans and Philistines all practiced augury in the eighth to sixth centuries BC. One of the most venerated augurs of history is the great Etruscan master Tages.

The term 'auspices' comes from the Latin *auspicious,* which means 'looking at birds'. Depending upon the types of birds and their movements and calls, the auspices from the gods may be favourable or unfavourable (auspicious or inauspicious). For Romans, augury is especially significant because it played a part in Rome's creation. Romulus and Remus, the founders of Rome, each performed auguries to divine the best location for their new city.

Roman practitioners report their findings to a magistrate. It is this judge who ultimately decides if the augury will be published or dismissed. The ancient Romans established rules and guidelines for the augurs. The reading of auspices was once an essential part of a broadly diverse Roman culture. Rulers depended upon the signs to make decisions. The devoutly religious and the superstitious all relied upon it as well, patricians and plebeians alike. Even the down-to-earth Stoics employed augurs, maintaining that if there are gods, they care for men, and that if they care for men they must send signs to men in order to guide them.

Over the development of the Roman empire, the definition of augury broadened to include other forms of divination. Haruspicy, which is the examination of the entrails of sacrificed birds and mammals, was learned from the Etruscans and quickly grew in popularity. Sadly, the augurs of today have mostly abandoned using the flights and calls of birds in favour of haruspicy for public divination.

Augury was already falling out of use by the first century BC. Political influences had created a taint of corruption, reducing the trust people had in the augurs. Leaders were less likely to employ them, and magistrates were less willing to support them. The stringent restraints upon who could perform augury led to many schools dying out, and the knowledge and practices along with them. The records were lost. The ancient science of the augurs faded into history.

Our thoughts:

It sounds as though the corruption and dissolution which overwhelmed the Roman Empire also brought the practice of augury to a near-end. As with much of the history of this time, there are many gaps in our knowledge. Little is known about the practice here in Roman Britannia, but perhaps it was not very different from what Master Occul is describing over in nearby Gaul.

Philippa

The fact that the history of divination begins with observation of the epic and extraordinary flight of birds, and ends in ritualised murder is, to me, a sure sign of decline and degradation.

Treya

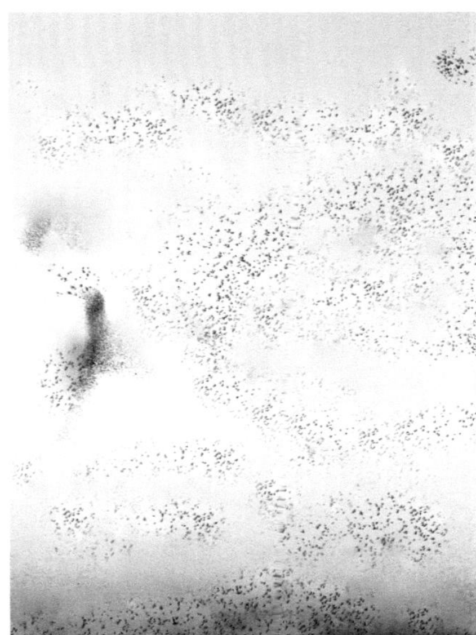

2. Feathers and flight- wing shape, airflow, group movement

Birds that show their auspices by flight are known as Alites. They are the elite masters of the air. Birds that reveal their auspices by their call are known as Oscines. Many birds belong to both the Alites and the Oscine categories. At their most orthodox, the Roman augurs only acknowledged eagles, vultures, and a few other species as being Alites.

Some practitioners refuse to acknowledge the flight patterns of certain birds because they were originally classified as Oscines and not Alites. This is wrong thinking. Anything larger than a hummingbird will create enough energy for divination to occur. The science of ornithomancy requires activity in the air. Only when the magnetic lines of the earth are engaged through flight will the augurs inquiries and intentions get to where they need to go.

The augur creates a viewing space called a templum, then observes whether the birds within the templum are moving as a group, acting independently, or some combination thereof. The augur should also observe the direction of the wind, and whether the birds are struggling, or are flowing with it. Alone or together, up and down, back and forth- all movements have implications. For the Romans, the high flight of birds (*praepes*) is an auspicious omen, the low flight less so (*infera*). Left to right movement indicates utilising instinct to guide reason. Right to left suggests employing reason to temper instinct.

Bird wings come in specialized forms that serve different functions. The augur should become familiar with them, and the way the air moves around them.

<u>Active soaring wings have a very long, slender shape</u>.
They are perfect for catching horizontal air currents, like sea breezes. They help minimize flapping to conserve energy, allowing the bird to travel over great distances. The long narrow wings allow the birds to soar, or fly without flapping, for a long time. These birds are much more dependent on wind currents than passive soaring birds.
Examples: albatross, gannet, gull

<u>Passive soaring wings appear wide and slotted</u>.
The spaces between the feathers aid the bird in catching thermal updrafts and soaring for long periods. This helps minimize flapping, conserving energy.
Examples: vulture, pelican, eagle

<u>Elliptical bird wings have a rounded appearance</u>.
They are good for quick maneuvers, take-offs, and turns, which is why they are often seen on birds that live in dense forests. Elliptical wings provide great agility and bursts of speed, but require lots of flapping to stay in flight.
Examples: dove, crow, robin

<u>High-speed bird wings are shorter than active or passive soaring wings</u>.
They are often pointed at the ends. To achieve rapid movement, the bird must spend lots of energy through flapping to reach high speeds. This makes these wings ideal for short bursts. Birds with this wingtype are very fast, but unlike those with elliptical wings, they can maintain their speed for a while.
Examples: falcon, tern, duck

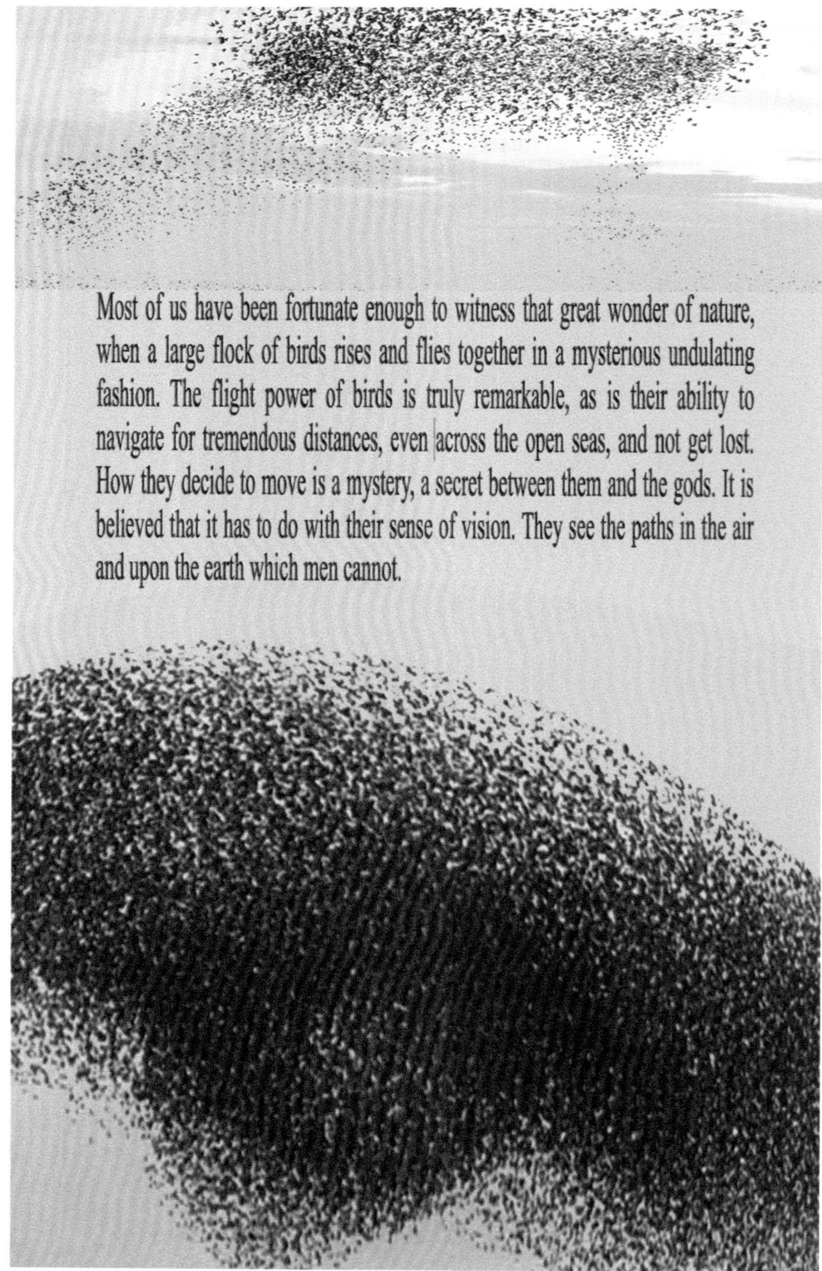

Most of us have been fortunate enough to witness that great wonder of nature, when a large flock of birds rises and flies together in a mysterious undulating fashion. The flight power of birds is truly remarkable, as is their ability to navigate for tremendous distances, even across the open seas, and not get lost. How they decide to move is a mystery, a secret between them and the gods. It is believed that it has to do with their sense of vision. They see the paths in the air and upon the earth which men cannot.

Our thoughts:

Once again, I agree with Master Occul. There's no reason that most birds shouldn't be considered both Oscines and Alites.

Philippa

There's a sense that some birds are not worthy of being considered as Alites.

To those people who would malign a species for being too small or common, I have one question-

Can you fly, unaided, through the air?

No, you cannot. So do not belittle the least of the birds. They are heirs to a power you will never have.

Treya

3. Tracking movement patterns- dexter, sinister, lagomorph, convex, concave, and mirrored

There is meaning in the way that birds move, individually or in a flock. In orthodox Roman augury, signs on the left (sinister) are generally considered lucky, while signs on the right (dexter) are often seen as unlucky. This is because the Roman augurs, when taking the auspices, face south, placing the east on their left and the west on their right. The east, associated with light and the rising sun, is deemed a more propitious direction than the west, which is linked to twilight and darkness. This is based on a limiting cultural bias, since augurs in other countries with much older traditions faced north. In truth, it makes no difference, as both north and south lie along the flow of the vertical magnetic lines of the earth. (For further information, see my treatise on the subject titled North Verses South- a Cultural Overview of Augury Alignments.)

Dexter is the right side, sinister is left. Lagomorph means moving shape. Concave means that the flock is curved down and away from you. Convex means they are curved toward the observer. Mirrored means that the movement is symmetrical, either horizontal, vertical or radial. A radial symmetry, like a flower blooming, is a rare and auspicious omen.

4. Directions of movement- left, right, up and down

The orthodox views also tend to oversimplify the properties of sinister and dexter by designating them as lucky and unlucky. The left actually represents intuition, instinct, the feminine divine, and passive creative energy. The right stands for reason, intellect, the power of the gods, and active creativity. A bird flying from left to right signifies the need for utilising instinct to guide reason. One travelling from right to left signifies the need of employing reason to temper instinct.

Our thoughts:

It is useful to consider this geometrically. When observing and recording the various positions and movements of birds, think of left and right as the horizontal axis, with up and down as the vertical. The vertical movement within the templum represents amplification. So, for example, if a bird goes from lower left to upper right, it might indicate that instinct needs to be informed by reason to a greater degree than if it had flown on the same level from left to right. The tendency toward reason or instinct may reflect the perspective of the querent as well as that of the augur.

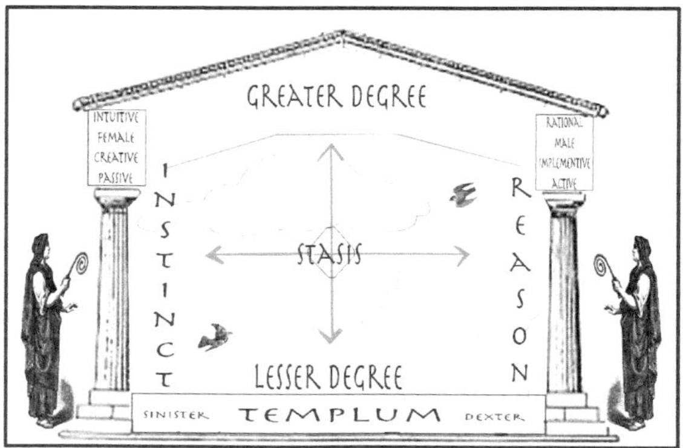

5. The birds-eye view- casting the attention upward and gazing down

This is not done during the actual augury, but in the advance preparation. The augur should practice this exercise on a regular basis, wherever there are birds flying overhead, as long as the environment is an appropriate and secure space. It is a casual exercise; there is no need for templum, robes, or lituus. Just look up and focus on a particular bird. The mind's attention should rise to travel with that bird. You should be able to see the ground stretched out below you, feel the force of the air and hear the whistle of the wind. It may help to close one's eyes and spread the arms wide when first learning the skill.

Our thoughts:

If you are in an open empty space, it's fun to spread your arms, close your eyes, and run along as if you are flying.

Philippa

Until you step in a hole and twist your ankle.

Treya

6. Templums and quadrants- using the lituus to apportion and examine the skies

The traditional Roman augur marks an area in the sky, known as a templum, while facing south. The templum refers to a space in the air which is bounded by imaginary lines. It is the framework through which the auspices are observed. The templum may also include a rectangular space on the ground, which has its boundaries marked by stationary objects that are announced aloud by the augur. In formal settings, a tent called a tabernaculum or templum-minus will be set up for the augury to take place within.

The lituus is the augur's wand. It is a staff with a spiral crook, used to divide the sky into quadrants and mark out the ritual space in the air. The passage of birds through this templum indicates divine favour or disfavour for a given undertaking. No two litui are the same, and the specific means of employing the divine tool for mapping and measuring varies according to the practitioner.

The lituus spiral is a manifestation of the Golden Mean. It is a two-dimensional polar coordinate system; a spiral in which the variable of the angle is inversely proportional to the square of the radius. The lituus is also employed as a symbol of office for the college of the augurs to mark them out as a priestly group.

For Romans, auspices need to be taken on Roman land. If the location is not Roman, it has to be consecrated before being used. Within Rome, already consecrated sites such as the Auguraculum on the Capitoline Hill are provided for auspices. In military camps, there is a designated area called the Augurale.

Our thoughts:

I would imagine that back in the year 11, Occul never considered the possibility that future readers of his book would no longer be living on Roman land!

Philippa

The idea that birds know or care about political boundaries is ridiculous. We do still consecrate the area before an augury, by singing chants and burning labdanum, cedar, and emmer.

Treya

Concerning the keeping of records:

Whilst in the field, it is useful to make quick notes and sketches. Enter the information later into your records. Do NOT bring your logbook into the countryside, or it is sure to get ruined.

Treya

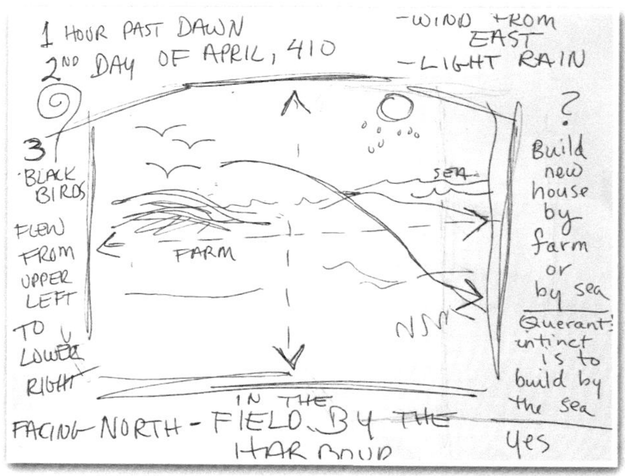

This example is from a query concerning where to build a new house. The querent was being advised to build near farmland, although what they really wanted was a seaside location. The spot chosen for divination covered both areas. The concluding interpretation was that they should trust their instincts, as the birds moved from upper left to lower right, and from land to water, indicating the increased need for the sinister instinct to guide the momentum of this project as it moved into the dexterous realm of active creation. The querent subsequently built the new home overlooking the harbour.

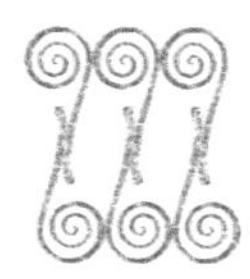

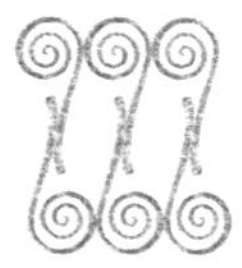

Philippa

Part Two- The Realm of the Birds

7. The Languages of Birds

The focus here will be on the cries of birds in conjunction with their movements through the templum. However, as with the bird's-eye view, listening to bird-calls is an easy and enjoyable exercise to practice on a regular basis. A familiarity with the various vocalisations will enhance the augur's experience. After a while, the listener begins to understand that what they are hearing are not mere isolated 'cries' of birds. There are patterns of call and response, with a rhythm and flow just like any conversation.

Birds communicate with their own kind, and with other kinds of birds. This interspecies communication helps them enhance their survival by ensuring a group response to shared threats, and by aiding them in finding resources more efficiently. Most birds coo, chirp, and trill when things are peaceful, and they shriek and squawk loudly when they are not. Mixed-species flocks use contact calls to maintain group cohesion and share information about food sources. An augur should be able to identify a species not just by sight, but also by the various calls that the birds use to communicate with, as well their meanings.

The calls of the sea birds- gulls, plovers, pipers and terns

These birds signal their presence by their calls. Sea-birds are social creatures, and their utterances are critical for group survival. Their piercing cries travel a long way through the air. They use different sounds for foraging, hunting, mating and parenting. A distress call will be repeated in an agitated manner, and passed along through the ranks very quickly.

For an augur, the cry of a sea-bird is a call to pay close attention.

The calls of the singing birds- larks, nightingales and moorhens

Birds sing to defend their territory. What may seem like a sweet sublime birdsong is just as likely to be an assertive territorial warning. They also sing to attract mates. Most song-birds have a complex and extensive repertoire of melodies. Birds from different species can communicate through alarm calls, which they learn by observing other species and associating their calls with danger.

There are many reasons for bird songs. Some reasons we understand, others we cannot fathom. We listen in amazement to their beautiful voices, with the awareness that even the most mundane-sounding call may represent a connection to the unseen realms of nature and the spirit world.

The calls of the small birds- sparrows, wrens, robins, and blackbirds

These common and highly communicative birds are associated with harvest, death omens, and the other realms of existence. Their vocals range from gentle cooing sounds to harsh trills, depending upon the species and the situation. Their common songs are familiar to us. Most of them have to do with mating, as these birds are prolific breeders. They choose to be around people, making the most of farmlands for food, and houses for shelter. Their calls signify domesticity, as well as green sorcery. Some believe that when certain of these birds sing, the fairy portals open.

The calls of the raptors- hawks, kites, and falcons

Raptors are often interpreted as messengers of divine guidance and wisdom. They are wise and observant fliers, and their calls contain pertinent information about the environment around them. Their voices may signify divine intervention, and the need for discernment, courage and focus. In Ancient Egypt, the hawk, or falcon, was a royal bird. Gods depicted as being hawk-headed, or accompanied by hawks, were Ra, Horus, Khensu, Ptah, Mentu, Rehu, Sokar & Keghsenuf. The hawk was also associated with the Great Mother Amenti.

Knowing when to flap and when to glide is crucial to a flying creature. Raptors know how to pace themselves while travelling through the air. For the augur, they symbolise focus, moderation, careful planning, and decisive action.

The calls of the unearthly birds- owls, lapwings, flageolets, and mockingbirds

In many instances, the unearthly birds are considered ominous, and a sure sign of impending bad luck or death. But that is just one aspect of the unearthly birds, and it distorts their position to focus so much on the morbid symbology.

The whistling, hooting, and other dramatic sounds emitted by these night-birds are surrounded in superstitions. They may be portents of danger. They are often linked to risky occupations like seafaring and mining, where the calls are believed to warn of danger or foretell loss of life.

Unearthly birds also include curlews, whimbrels, golden plovers, lapwings, and swifts.

Owls are often associated with wisdom, knowledge, and insight, particularly in Western cultures, due to their nocturnal habits and association with the goddess Athena. However, their symbolism can also include darker aspects like death or misfortune, depending on the culture and context. Their nocturnal nature and keen eyesight are linked to intuition and the ability to perceive hidden truths or insights. Owls can represent the ability to transform and adapt to change, often symbolised by their ability to change direction mid-flight.

Night-birds are often heard and not seen, so we rely upon their cries more than the other birds. Which bring us to the mockingbird. Mockingbirds, as well as several other species, copy the sounds of other birds. The astute listener may try to detect the fraud, but even the birds themselves are fooled by the skilled mimic. The augur should not worry about the subterfuge; the type of cry matters more here than who it was uttered by.

HERMES

THOTH
HORUS

The calls of the growling birds- jays, jackdaws, magpies, crows, and ravens

The growling birds are believed to act as messengers between the physical and spiritual worlds, carrying offerings to the gods and ancestors. Of all the birds, these are the ones who will actually speak to humans. The two ravens, Hugin (thought) and Munin (memory), fly across the world each day, gathering information for Odin. Odin's ravens are a symbol of his wisdom, intelligence, and ability to see all that is happening in the world.

In Celtic mythology, ravens are associated with goddesses such as the Morrigan, the goddess of war and fate, who took the form of a raven on battlefields. The presence of ravens could be an omen of death or a sign of a goddess's presence. Ravens may also be seen as guardians or wise beings, like the ravens of the Welsh god Bran the Blessed. Because ravens and crows are also the messengers and tricksters of the bird kingdom, they are special to Hermes/ Mercury. In Hibernian, Cymraeg, Kernowek, and Gallic folklore, the raven and crow are strongly associated with Lugh (also known as Lugus, the patron of our great Roman city of Lugdunum). These birds are not just his sacred animals but also represent his connection to magic, prophecy, and wisdom.

The growling birds are often associated with prophecy and knowledge, reflecting their keen observation of their surroundings. They are some of the most clever animals on the earth, smarter than any dog, able to solve complex problems and use simple tools which they devise themselves. They can open and close latches, and they will drop hard nuts onto the road so that wagon wheels will crush them and they can get the nut meat. They can have a special and even close relationship with people. Birds such as magpies and jackdaws are well-known collectors/thieves of human items such as jewellery, combs, buttons, coins and even clothing.

Growling birds do more than growl; they have an extraordinarily wide repertoire of squawks, caws, chirps and growls, each with a different meaning. The individual sounds may be combined to form long sentences and complex ideas. The augur should listen for begging calls, alert cries, and calls for social interaction. And, if the listener is fortunate, the occasional human word or phrase.

Our thoughts:

We once visited a cafe in Plympton where there was a pet crow. His name was Order-up, because that is what he would squawk whenever the cook rang the bell to alert the servers. He sat on a counter by the til, hailing arriving customers with "Sit'n'eat!" and saying "Combach-tzoon!" as they departed. In between, he muttered, groomed himself, ate bread, cheese and butter, and drank watered-

down ale. He was a real charmer. He never missed a chance to hail and farewell a customer.

Philippa

Order-up! It sounded more like 'order-ack'. What a character. He collected trinkets, and he'd keep them on the counter, moving them around in an ever-changing display. People gave him bits of jewellery and shiny things. He actually brought in quite a profit for the owner. He had his own bowl of coins. The owner had trained him to pick out coins to make change. He'd pick up a coin in his beak, drop it on the counter, and slide it over to the customer. Then he would cock his head sweetly, looking plaintively at the coin, then at the customer. They would be so charmed that most would suggest that he keep the coin, at which point he would slide it until it wedged up again the edge of the counter and he could get his beak around it. Then he would drop it back into his coin-stash with a satisfied look, turning his head to listen to the sound of it as it landed in the bowl.

Treya

8. The Exalted Realm of the Death Eaters- buzzards and vultures

Throughout human history, vultures have been considered sacred symbols of purification, rebirth, and alchemical transformation by many cultures in different historical periods. The idea of purification associated with vultures is present in many myths and religions, and in the burial practices of ancient populations. The purification symbology derives from the fact that carrion birds do not prey upon living animals, and they are able to consume diseased and rotting flesh with no ill effects.

Vultures are associated with death, but also life and birth. The Egyptian word for mother contains the vulture hieroglyph. They were conspicuous in all the ancient Mediterranean civilisations, and especially revered by Egyptians. Vultures are considered sacred to Ares/Mars since they feed on the decay after a bloody battle.

Thalia was a lover of Zeus from Sicily, who gave birth to the twin Daemons called the Plaice, after Zeus came to her in the guise of a vulture.

No culture embraces the vulture more than Rome. One of the most famous auspices is the one which is connected with the founding of Rome itself. When they arrived at the Palatine Hill, the twins Remus and Romulus argued over where the exact position of the city should be. Romulus was set on building the city upon the Palatine, but Remus wanted to build the city on the strategic and easily fortified Aventine Hill.

The two agreed to settle their argument by testing their abilities as augurs. Each took a seat on the ground apart from one another, and, according to Plutarch, Remus saw six vultures, after which Romulus saw twelve. The two clashed over whether the preference of the gods was indicated by Remus seeing vultures before Romulus did, or by Romulus seeing twelve vultures while Remus saw only six.

Vultures were pre-eminent in Roman augury, furnishing the strongest signs an augur could receive from a wild bird. They were considered sacred birds, and were protected by law.

Our thoughts:

Romulus and Remus may have been critical to the history of Rome, but they were crude and narrow-minded practitioners of augury.

Philippa

Truly! Eighteen vultures would surely have been a sign of abundance and success enough for all parties. Unless they were looking for a fight to begin with.

Treya

9. The Supreme Rulers of the Sky- eagles and their portents

The eagle is a the herald of the Nile, and the royal bird of the Thebans. It is used in hieroglyphics as the symbol for the letter A.

The eagle represents wisdom and light. Some believe that the flapping of eagle's wings cause the storms of the sky-god to manifest in the world.

Eagles are associated with sky-gods and represent spiritual power, majesty, victory and ascension in many different cultures. The Cymraeg name for the mountains of Snowdonia is Eryri, from the word for eagle (eryr), meaning 'abode of the eagles'. In Norse mythology, on the topmost branch of the world tree Yggdrasil (a giant Ash tree, also known as the tree of life), there sits an Eagle. On the beak of the eagle, between its eyes, there sits a falcon. Between the two of them, they represent the spectrum of avian potential.

The call of the eagle resonates with glory, might and sublime energy. It is the sound of divine justice and spiritual awakening.

The eagle has been the universal symbol of Rome from its earliest days as a republic. Traditionally, when a Caesar dies, he is cremated, and an eagle is set free amongst the flames, so that it might escort the emperor's soul to the heavenly realms. It is the bird associated with Zeus/Jupiter, the king of the gods, and Jove is often seen in the company of a mighty eagle. The Roman legions march under the standard of a silver eagle with outstretched wings, clutching a thunderbolt.

Eagle and Crow constellations.

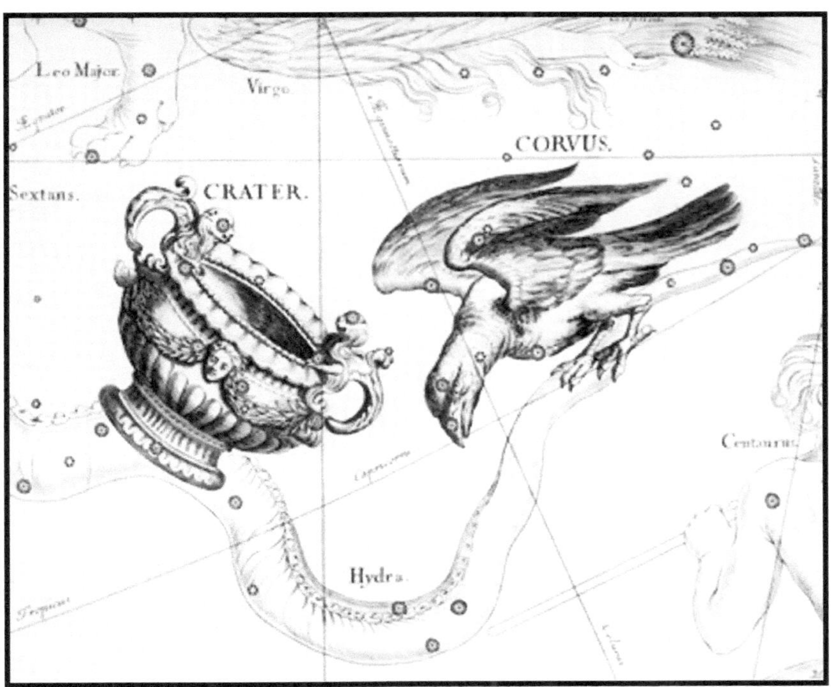

10. The birds and the cosmos-

Birds are associated with the visible dome of the sky, of course. But they are also affected by the pull of the planets and the moon, and guided by sun, stars, and the magnetic lines of the earth.

Birds use the sun's position to maintain a consistent heading during the day, especially during a migration. Migration is a very dynamic activity. Migratory birds within the templum can add another dimension of meaning to the augur's interpretation.

The lunar cycle influences the activity of certain nocturnal birds, affecting when they hunt or migrate, particularly during full moons when there is more light. Night-time augury involves watching nocturnal birds in flight, interpreting sounds, or otherwise observing their behaviour to discern omens. The practice of night-augury may also be connected to the augur's dream-life, if they are that sort of seer.

Many of the known constellations represent birds, and there have always been strong ties between ornithomancers and astronomers. Birds use constellations and the position of specific stars to navigate at night, especially during long-distance migrations. They not only use the stars for reference, but they are adept at compensating for the latitudinal seasonal shift of the skies.

Birds possess an internal sense of direction, a special connection between their eyes and brain, that allows them to sense the Earth's magnetic field, helping them navigate even when visual cues are obscured.

11. What birds see and hear- beyond the human spectra

Birds can see the lines of the air, and the earth's magnetic pathways. Their eyes can detect the high vibrations of purple light, which human eyes cannot.

It would very likely drive us mad, to see the world as it truly is: full of vibrating magnetic lines travelling like lightning through the ethers upon waves of cosmic purple energy.

Birds also have the ability to hear frequencies well beyond the range of humans, both low and high. When the gods speak, we do not hear it, but they do, and they share that information with us.

It is our job to learn to properly divine the message and meaning.

Part Three- Principles of Augury

12. Augury: magical divination, or mere natural observation?

Why do birds fly? Some people think that they are the messengers of the gods, and that is why they fly. Others are more inclined towards a rational scientific explanation, such as the theory that birds developed from dragons, or some other prehistoric flying beast. The two ideas are not mutually exclusive, and there is no reason that both approaches cannot be considered simultaneously. Augury is the science of natural observation as well as the art of divination.

13. Recognising patterns- seasonal, annual, and epochal

All the movements and sounds made by birds have different meanings and interpretations according to their different circumstances, and to the time of the year when observations are made. The importance of keeping a journal cannot be overstressed. It is by utilising the record that patterns are detected. Some of these patterns, such as seasonal migration, are predictable, and happen in a relatively short amount of time. Other, larger patterns only emerge after many years and even after many generations. But only if the records have been preserved.

14. Messages from the Gods- blessings, prophecies and warnings

Augury began as the study of birds in the air. The term was eventually applied to all the divination techniques, including aeromancy (interpreting atmospheric phenomena), haruspicy (the study of entrails), hepatoscopy (the interpretation of dissected livers), the incidents of animals walking inadvertently onto the augur's ground, and the movement of ground-birds in response to being fed.

None of these take place in the air, therefore they do not meet the standards for true augury. The one exception is aeromancy, or divination by storm, which also has its roots in very ancient times. The observations and interpretations of cosmic thunder and lightning represent the maximum auspicium sent by Jupiter. The nature of the omen is decided based on what direction lightning came from. Aeromancers meticulously observe and record weather patterns, including the direction and intensity of storms, the types of clouds, and the sounds of thunder, to discern their significance.

The Fallacious Role of Ground-Birds

There have been some very foolish approaches to divination by bird observation. One of them is called 'auspicia ex tripudiis', literally 'auspiciousness from dancing', which consists of observing the eating behaviour of the sacred hens. When the time for divination comes, the keeper releases the chickens and throws bread or cake at them. If the chickens refuse to come out and eat, cry out, or beat their wings, the signs are considered inauspicious.

But, if a chicken leaves its cage to eat, and drops food from its mouth, as birds tend to do, it is considered to be a favourable sign. When the sacred chickens rush back to pick up the grains that fell out of their beaks while eating, it is read as the most favourable prophecy (tripudium solistimum).

These ground-birds are bred specially for this purpose, kept in captivity, clipped and robbed of flight, and often overfed or starved to influence the outcome of the augury. This type of trick is easier to carry out than actual divination – there is no need to have to go forth into the forests, hills and wetlands, and seek out the birds as they are in their own realm. Sitting around and feeding captive chickens is much easier.

Eventually, the term augury expanded to include terrestrial animal behaviours, signs such as a falling branch, a gust of wind, and even randomly spoken words. Some of these other forms of divination might have some limited and local value, or meaningful social and ritual uses. But I dismiss this 'chicken dance' approach to the practice as nothing but superstitious nonsense and systemised fraud perpetuated by the lazy and ignorant. It's one of the things that led to the augur losing status in Roman society.

15. 'Sort Sol' - The black sun, good or bad omen?

This phenomenon occurs when there are so many birds flying in one disc-shaped mass that they fill the sky and eclipse the sun. There are those that swear it is a bad omen, while some think otherwise. The fact is, the black sun has no intrinsic divining properties, but should be viewed in context like any other movement.

16. Auguries of the future- portents, divinations and petitions

There are two official classifications of portents; impetrative (impetrativa, sought or requested) and oblative (oblativa, unsought or offered). Impetrativa are signs given in conjunction with the augur's intention and interpretation. Oblativa are the unexpected and unsought events and interruptions which may happen during the auspices. Impetrativa and oblativa may also occur while the magistrate is reviewing the merit or significance of an interpretation.

The Roman priestly augurs are meant to be unbiased. They are expected to give the same amount of attention and care to every petition, no matter how monumental or inconsequential. Although augurs have the power to interpret the signs, it is ultimately the responsibility of the Roman magistrate to execute consequent decisions, or withhold or debate judgment as to future plans. The magistrates are expected to understand the basics of divination as they pertain to public business.

17. Wearing the hood- protocols for interacting with officials, and with the public

The story of augury did not begin with Rome. However, most of what we know about augury comes from Roman documents.

The Roman augurs typically wear the traditional hooded praetexta, a garment worn over a tunic with two broad, vertical purple stripes, and distinguished by a broad purple stripe on its border. It is a symbol of authority and status. In less formal, and in military settings, they will wear the trabea, a simpler robe of state. They carry the spiral lituus and a capis, a one handled offering-bowl.

At its height, there was a great deal of pressure and responsibility put upon the practitioners of augury. Everyone wanted results, and sometime the consequences of a discredited interpretation could be dire, both for the client, and for the unlucky augur. If an augur committed an error in the interpretation of the vitia (signs), it might be considered offensive to the gods and potentially have disastrous effects unless corrected. Elections, passing laws, and starting wars were all delayed until there was assurance of divine approval.

At the height of the empire, the Roman College of Augurs was wealthy and powerful. They even minted their own coins, often featuring the lituus and capis. They were protective of their members, who were often vulnerable to vengeance from the rulers and the wrath of the public. The College in Lugdunum is still taking care of its augurs. We will provide an advocatus if needed, to plead for a practitioner in court. The College also has a private security force, the templum custodes, to protect the members from threats of retribution and attempts at coercion.

Augury was ubiquitous back then. Augurs kept books containing records of past signs, rituals, prayers, and other resources to help other augurs, and for governing officials to understand the fundamentals of augury. Sadly, there was a great temptation to meddle with the authenticity of the auspicious. Although most augurs were honourable, there were enough corrupt practitioners to taint the public's view of the practice, when led to its decline.

In modern times of course, there is much less pressure on the augur from the public or the ruling class. The role of the diviner has shrunk considerably, becoming more personal and less formal. Here in Gaul, many of the official practices have devolved into superstition. The augury we know and respect from old is now more often a folk-practice than an official event. One one hand, it is too bad that traditions have been lost, but on the other, it is good that it allows for augury to now be practiced by a much broader and diverse group of people. Even some of the wise-women in our province have found roles as sky-diviners. Some of the local officials don't entirely approve, but the greater community does, and all of our augurs are upstanding and productive citizens who serve with integrity and give generously to local charities.

Gone is the time when everyone knew and respected the augurs. These days, we are often met with curiosity and even derision. The lituus is still employed, but the priestly garments of late are often simply a striped purple scarf or stole, which draws less attention than full robes. However, there is currently a colourful and exciting trend towards more elaborate Etruscan-style augur's garments, as an attractive alternative to traditional Roman augur robes and their potential negative associations.

It is essential to deal with the public diplomatically. No matter how large or small your scope and influence, when you are 'wearing the hood', you are representing an ancient and venerated tradition, and should behave accordingly. You are the connection between humanity and the divine messengers of the gods. Every encounter is an opportunity to help another person become closer to the divine, and to learn to venerate the birds of the air.

Finis.

Our thoughts:

What Master Occul says is reassuring. If he were here, I would thank him for his support. As females, we wouldn't have had a chance of being augurs back in the old days. We probably still wouldn't, in most places.

As we often explain to curious onlookers, augury is more about making informed deductions based on observations of the natural world than it is about fortune-telling. I like to think that Master Occul would approve of that interpretation.

Philippa

Master Occul is so wise and inspiring. He makes me believe that as long as you work hard, speak thoughtfully, show true compassion, and always strive for greater understanding, the powers of the air will reward your efforts with successful divinations.

Treya

Occulus Praefectus Augures

THE BIRDS

Aristophanes wrote 'The Birds' in 414 BC.
It is a delightful fantasy, rich in avian symbolism.
It is also a political satirization of the Athenian government and its policies.

"We are your oracles—your Ammon, Delphi, Dodona, and your Apollo. You don't start on anything without first consulting the birds, whether it's about business affairs, making a living, or getting married. Every prophecy that involves a decision you classify as a bird... so clearly, we are your gods of prophecy."

Prometheus is a Titan. In Greek mythology, he is known for his kindness to humans.

He created mankind, and then he brought gifts of knowledge to humanity. For that, he was famously punished by Zeus, having his liver perpetually plucked out and eaten by a raptor.

According to Aeschylus, Prometheus introduced ornithomancy to humans, and taught them to observe avian behaviors.

Prometheus is also credited with teaching mathematics, medicine, agriculture, and writing.

From ancient Athens, this Attic-ware platter shows Prometheus and the Goddess Hera, and displays the symbolic relationship between the lituus and the lotus. Attributed to the artist Douris.

Cicero's two volume treatise 'De Divinatione', from the first century BC, has been a valuable resource for the study of ancient divinatory practices.

Although Cicero is a rationalist who does not trust divination to be wholly reliable, he considers it to be an art, regardless of the success or failure of the outcome. He compares it to medicine, which might not always cure, but is still a valid skill to practice.

He describes two types of augury. The more credible path involves learning the art of deduction based on observation. The other, which relies upon dreams or trances, is considered to be 'devoid of art'.

CASSANDRA

Cassandra, a royal princess of Troy, was granted the gift of prophecy by Apollo in exchange for her love.

The story involves a snake licking her ears, which granted her the power to understand the language of birds.

She later refused Apollo's advances, leading him to curse her, so that her warnings about the future were never believed.

The reptilian snake and the avian bird motifs mirror one another.

They represent opposing forces of life, as in the World Tree where birds live in the crown and snakes in the roots.

ANCIENT STATUES
THE EARLIEST IMAGES OF AUGURS

ROMAN
AUGUR
COINS

GLOSSARY

College of the Augurs - the priestly guild of Roman ornithomancers
Occulus Praefectus Augures - head of the Lugdunum College of Augury
Ornithomancy - bird augury, from Greek 'ornis', fowl and 'manteia', divination
Magistrate - Roman judge who ultimately decided if the augury would be published or dismissed.
Auspice - 'looking at birds' for favourable or unfavourable signs (auspicious or inauspicious).
Dexter - right side
Sinister - left side
Lagomorph - moving shape
Templum - the space in the sky marked off by imaginary lines
Augury - the study of divination
Aeromancy - interpreting atmospheric phenomena
Haruspicy - the study of entrails
Hepatoscopy - the study of dissected livers
Tripudium solistimum - most favourable prophecy
Auspicia ex tripudiis - 'auspiciousness from dancing', the chicken dance
Hibernian, Cymraeg, Kernowek & Gallic- Irish, Welsh, Cornish & French
Praetexta - a Roman garment worn over a tunic with two broad, vertical purple stripes, and distinguished by a broad purple stripe on its border.
Trabea - a simple robe of state
Lituus - spiral wand of the augurs
Capis - a one handled bowl
Impetrative - impetrativa, a sought or requested omen
Oblative - oblativa, unsought or offered omens
Sort Sol - The black sun, the phenomenon which occurs when there are so many birds flying in one disc shaped mass that they fill the sky and eclipse the sun
Plympton - Plymouth, England
Mons Relaxus - Morlaix, Brittany, France
Uxantis - Channel Isle of Ushant, Ile d'Ouessant
Bades - Channel Isle, Bréhatle de Batz
Glénan - Channel Island

Queries from Practitioners and Notes on Record Keeping

- **If a man-made object such as a kite appears in my templum, should I try to ignore it?**

Man-made objects represent technology. You are wondering how that might affect your interpretation, if at all. Their sightings might in fact refer specifically to something technical or mechanical, but it's just as likely that they represent the concept of control: control of an environment, or in the manipulation of a certain space.
Are the birds ignoring the man-made object? If so, you should as well. It will have no effect on your augured interpretation. But if the birds respond to it, pay attention to whether they seem threatened by it or not. If they do, it may be a sign that the success of a particular event may be impeded by technology.
If the birds flee from it, or seem bothered by it, watch and see if the flying object is growing larger as it gets closer, or shrinking as it travels away.
If it is diminishing, it might indicate that the project or event in question is affected by a lack of appropriate technology or by technology which is outdated, malfunctioning or underperforming
If the birds flee or are bothered, and the object grows closer, it may indicate that there is a danger from technology being misused, overwhelming, or dangerous.

Philippa

As ever, it all depends upon the birds. If there is no bird in your templum, just the man-made object, there is no meaning. Even with birds present, non-ornithopteric objects such as loose bits of clothing or flying leaves have no meaning, only those being controlled by people.

Treya

- **Where I live, there are flocks of various types of birds. Some of them don't fly at all. I'm not sure if that's just the way they are made, or if they have been bred that way. My question is, supposing one lived in a place where no birds flew at all. Is it possible to perform an augury with grounded birds?**

With respect to all the lovely ground-birds, they are of no use for augury, despite a long and storied reputation. Really, it's about what birds do, which is fly, not what they are. It is their propulsion through the space of the templum that sets the augury in motion. The movement creates waves, which combine with the intentions of the augur, and radiate outward, like ripples in a pond. That's why discovering the optimum height for the templum is important.

Too low to the ground, and the ripples may not gain momentum, or they might be impeded. They need the space to grow in strength. But too high, and they become thin and stretched, losing their potency.

Treya

It's a curious question. If I lived in a place where no birds flew, I don't think I would need an augur to divine that something was amiss!

Philippa

- **What does it mean when a bird in my templum poops?**

I think that we may safely assume that it is of no consequence if a bird poops in your templum.

Treya

Unless of course you happened to be standing directly below at the time, in which case it is actually auspicious. As an augur, getting your head pooped on is a blessing and a fortunate portent.

Philippa

- **I was at the river recently, trying some augury. There were birds of every kind flying through my templum, hundreds of them, going every which way. How is so much activity to be interpreted?**

I'm not exactly sure, but it seems auspicious. Perhaps it is a portent of upcoming abundance.

Philippa

It's nice to think that it's a positive sign, but with so much chaotic activity, it may be also be a warning against excess or too much ambition.

Treya

- **How do you decide where to practice? Are there better spots than others?**

If you have the accessibility, the site of the augury should resonate with the question. For example, a client recently came to us, concerned about an upcoming journey by ship. The woman in question needed to travel from Plympton, in Britannia Sud, across the channel to Mons Relaxus in Brittany. She was concerned, as she was terrified of sea travel, and tended to panic when out of sight of land.

We went down to the harbour, and created a templum looking towards Gaul. A crow appeared. It had hopped up onto the harbour wall nearest to us. It then flew partly across the water and landed on a rocky outcropping. It stopped for a moment, then took wing again, flying in another short burst to a small brushy island, where it landed on a tree branch. Another short flight took it to a wooden pylon, where it clung briefly before flying the rest of the way. It landed safely on the sea wall on the other side of the harbour.

Philippa

Our advice to the client was to break the journey up into short trips from island to island, so that she would be less affected by so much time on the open sea. She took our recommendation, stopping at Uxantis, Ushant (Ile d'Ouessant), Bades, Bréhatle de Batz, and the Glénan Islands. It took longer than it might have otherwise, and was a far more circuitous route, but she was very satisfied with the outcome, as her health remained intact.

Treya

THE STUDY OF RECORDED FLOCK MOVEMENTS OVER THE LANDSCAPE IS BASED ON OBSERVATIONAL TALLIES MADE BY THE SKY-WATCHING COMMUNITY.
LARGER SYMBOLS REPRESENT LARGER FLOCKS. ARROWS INDICATE DIRECTION.

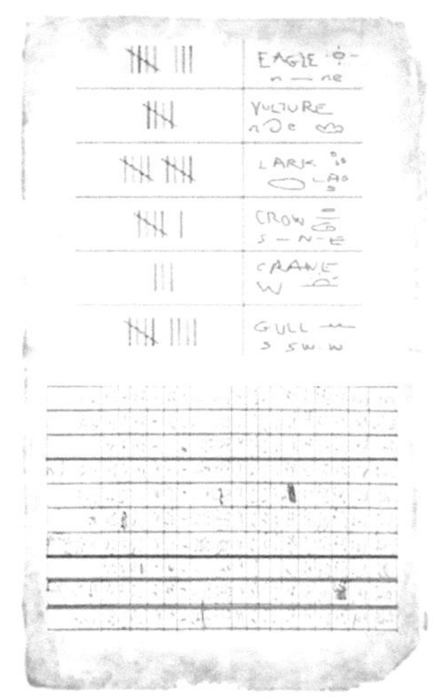

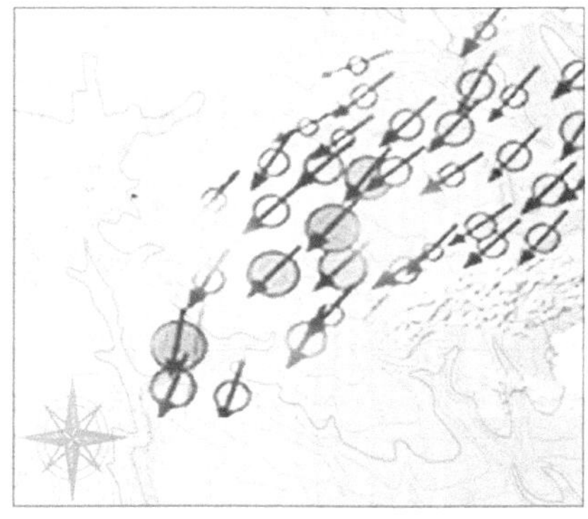

RECORDED OBSERVATIONS MAY BE SIMPLE OR COMPLEX

RECORDS MAY APPEAR TO BE CRYPTIC, BUT THAT DOESN'T MATTER, AS LONG AS THEY MAKE SENSE TO THE RECORD KEEPERS.

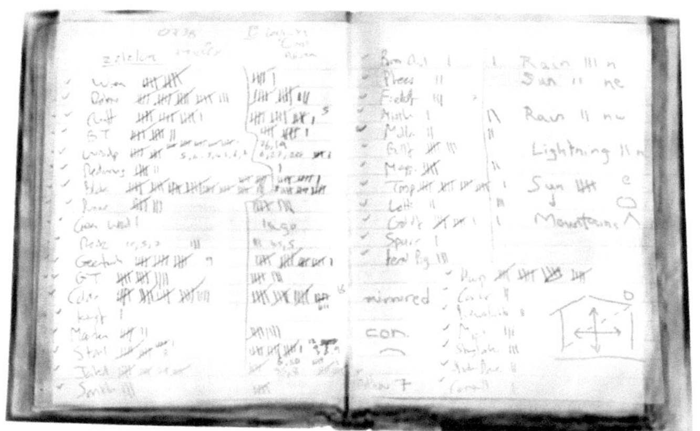

YEARLY DATA MAY BE SUPER-IMPOSED

UPON THE WHEEL OF THE HEAVENS

A RECORD OF TERNS FLYING BY THE RIVER DURING THE YEAR OF 408 AD.

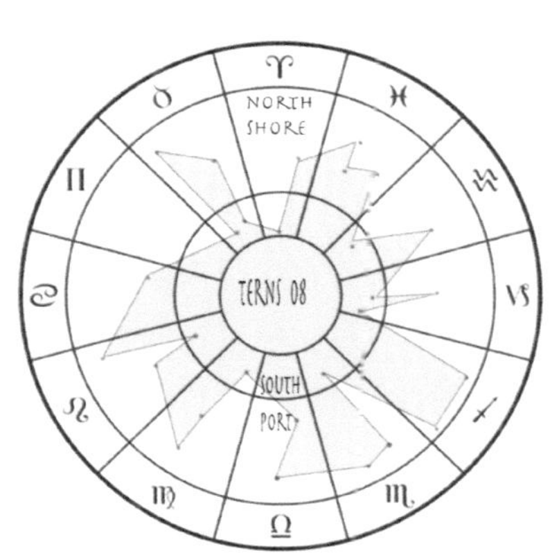

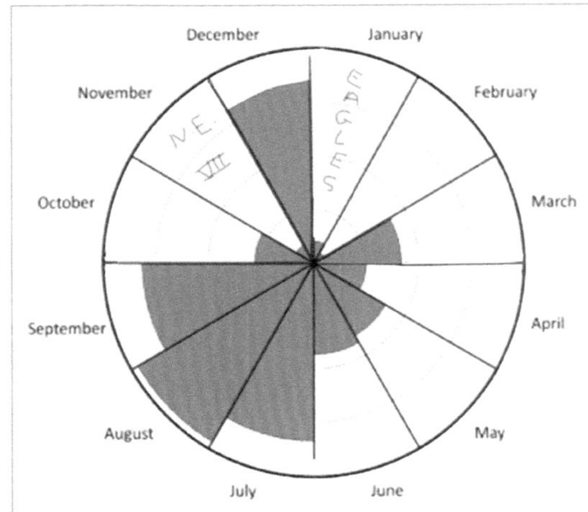

A RECORD OF EAGLES SPOTTED IN THE NORTH-EAST FIELD DURING THE YEAR OF 410 AD.

AUGURY AND GEOMANCY

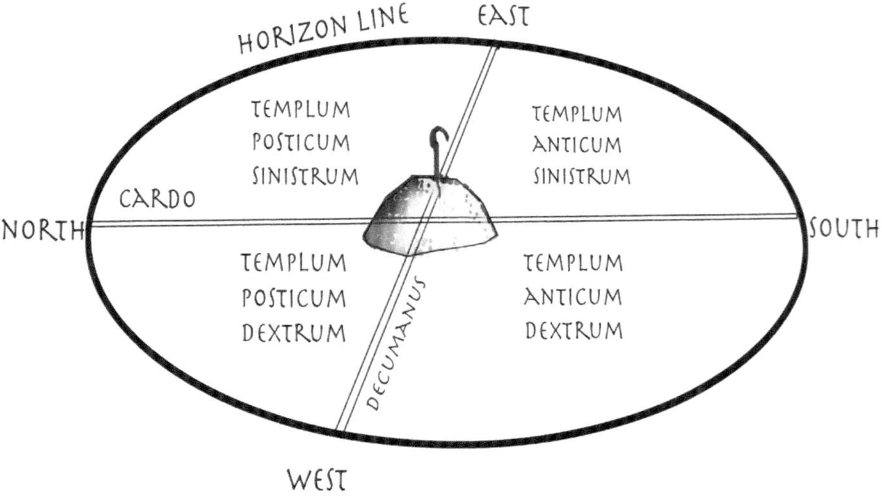

THIS DIAGRAM REPRESENTS AN ETRUSCAN-STYLE AUGURY, PERFORMED TO PLAN OUT A CITY OR TEMPLE COMPLEX.

THE AUGURY TAKES PLACE ON THE OMPHALOS, THE RAISED MOUND IN THE CENTRE OF THE ELLIPSE.

THE DESIGNATIONS ARE TEMPLUM BACK RIGHT, TEMPLUM FRONT RIGHT, TEMPLUM BACK LEFT AND TEMPLUM FRONT LEFT.

CARDO IS A PIVOT LINE, AND DECUMANUS REFERS TO THE EAST-WEST GRID LAYOUT AND ITS MEASUREMENT.

GEOMANCY IS A FORM OF EARTH DIVINATION, OFTEN PAIRED WITH BIRD AUGURY. IT IS USED TO INTERPRET THE FEATURES OF THE LANDSCAPE TO CREATE AN AUSPICIOUS PLAN FOR BUILDING AND DEVELOPING AN AREA.

PIPPA AGRIPPA IN BRITANNIA PRIMA
AN TIR GALLÓSEK: THE MIGHTY LAND
BOOK ONE
MARIA KAY ANTHONY
MARCUS CONSTANTINIDES IN ALBION SUB TERRA
AN TIR GALLOSEK: THE MIGHTY LAND
BOOK TWO
MARIA KAY ANTHONY
TREYA MEYNACK
WESTERN AIR
MARIA KAY ANTHONY

Borlowan
Books

AN TIR GALLÓSEK
THE MIGHTY LAND
A THREE VOLUME NOVEL
BY MARIA KAY ANTHONY
BORLOWAN
BOOKS

Maria Kay Anthony lives with her husband in the countryside near Lawrence, Kansas. She enjoys travelling, writing, singing, studying, gardening, nature-watching, creating art, and making music.

Journal Pages and Excerpts

TECHNIQUES AND TOOLS FOR RECORD KEEPING

AN EXAMPLE OF BIRD RECORDING, INCLUDING TYPE, COUNT, MOVEMENT, SOUND AND WEATHER CONDITIONS. THE BIRD-COUNT IS OF IMPORT TO THOSE WHO COMBINE NUMEROLOGY WITH AUGURY. IT IS ALSO USEFUL TO NATURALISTS AND WEATHER-WATCHERS.

BIRD TALLY CHART — MONTH ______ YEAR ______

TYPE OF BIRD	TALLY MARKS (BUNDLES OF 𝍸)	TOTAL
SWALLOW	𝍸 𝍸 𝍸 𝍸 𝍸 IIII	XXIX
	SW TO NE/LAGOMORPH/LOUD CHATTER	LIGHT RAIN

EACH AUGUR MAY FIND THEIR OWN BEST WAY OF RECORD KEEPING. THIS FORMAT IS EASILY READABLE AND USEFUL TO SHARE WITH OTHER PRACTITIONERS.

PHENOLOGY IS THE STUDY OF THE CYCLICAL PASSING OF TIME IN RELATION TO NATURE AND THE STARS. AS SEEN IN THE EXAMPLES, THE PHENOLOGY WHEEL MAY BE REPRESENTED BY THE MONTHS, THE SEASONS, OR BY THE SIGNS OF THE ZODIAC.

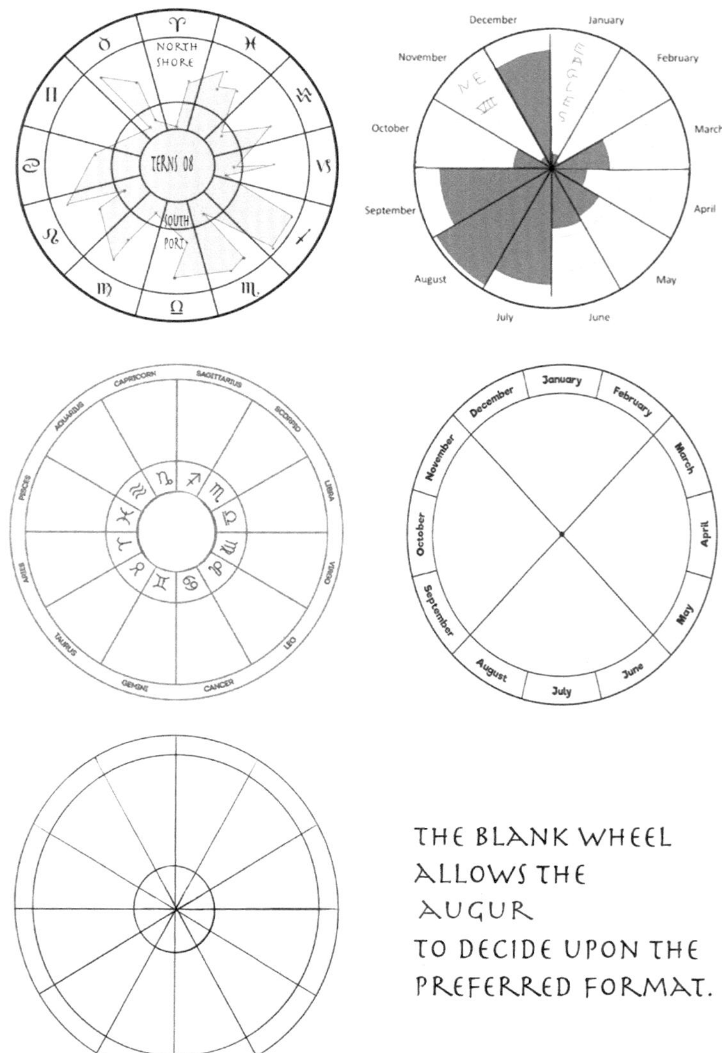

THE BLANK WHEEL ALLOWS THE AUGUR TO DECIDE UPON THE PREFERRED FORMAT.

BIRD TALLY CHART

MONTH ________

YEAR ________

TYPE OF BIRD	TALLY MARKS (BUNDLES OF 𝍸)	TOTAL

BIRD TALLY CHART

MONTH ________
YEAR ________

TYPE OF BIRD	TALLY MARKS (BUNDLES OF 𝍸)	TOTAL

BIRD TALLY CHART

MONTH ________
YEAR ________

TYPE OF BIRD	TALLY MARKS (BUNDLES OF 𝍸)	TOTAL

BIRD TALLY CHART

MONTH ________
YEAR ________

TYPE OF BIRD	TALLY MARKS (BUNDLES OF 𝍸)	TOTAL

BIRD TALLY CHART

MONTH ________
YEAR ________

TYPE OF BIRD	TALLY MARKS (BUNDLES OF 卌)	TOTAL

BIRD TALLY CHART

MONTH ________
YEAR ________

TYPE OF BIRD	TALLY MARKS (BUNDLES OF 卌)	TOTAL

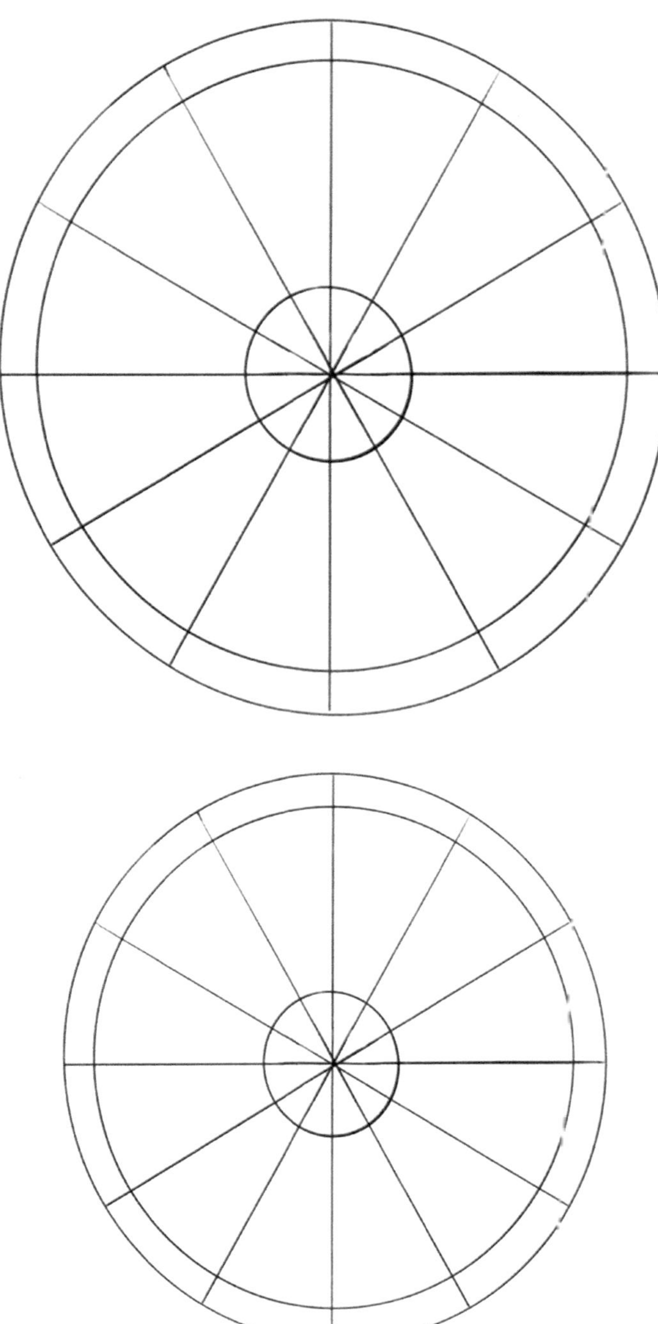

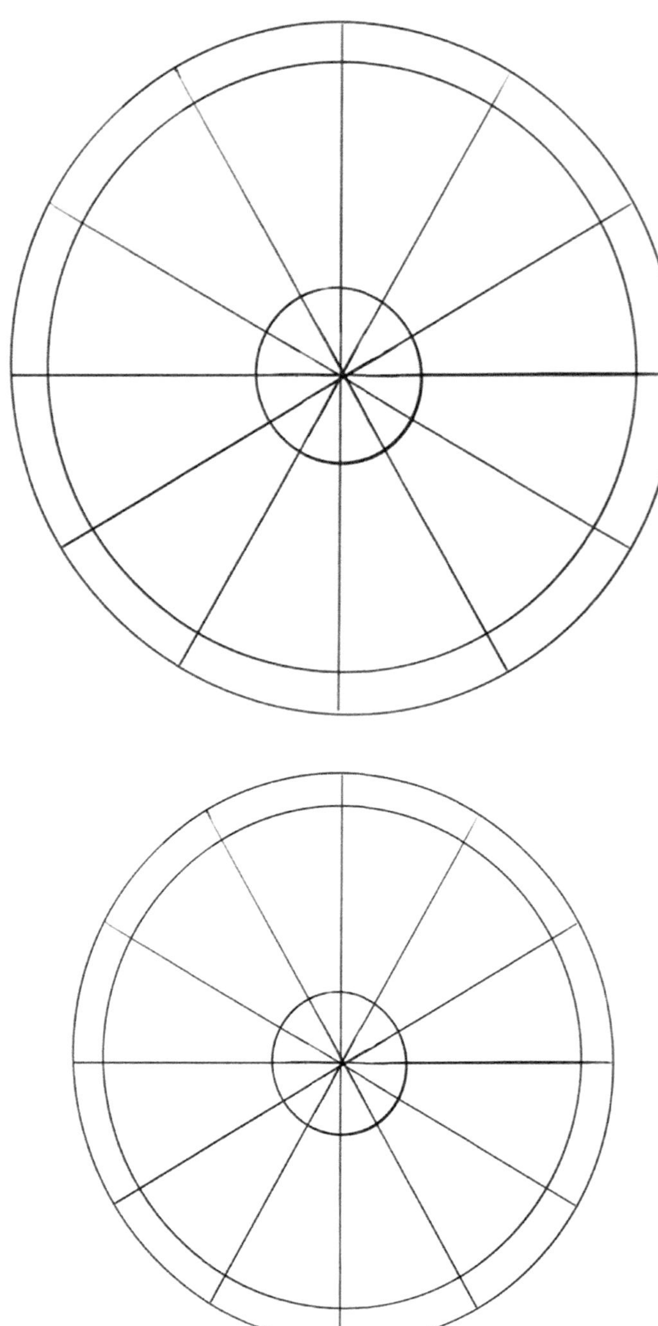

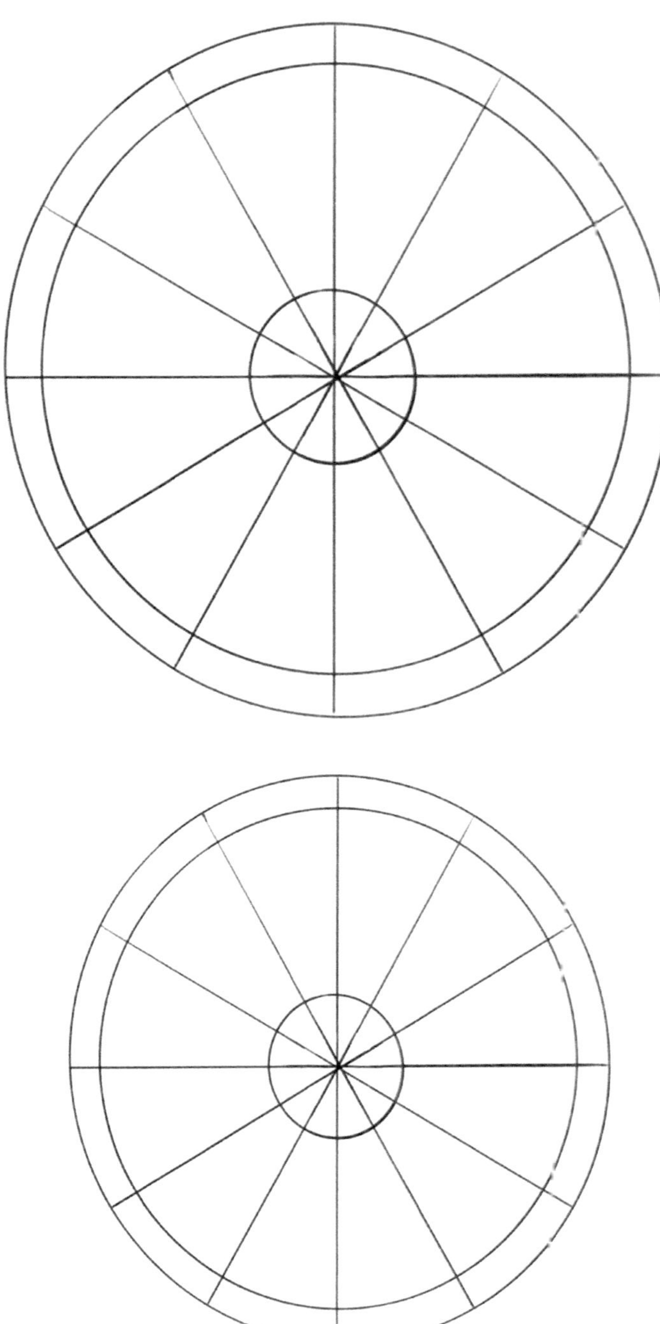

AUGURS IN ACTION - SELECTED EXCERPTS

(AUGUR - A DIVINER WHO WATCHES FLOCKS OF BIRDS)

FROM THE INTRODUCTION TO AN TIR GALLÓSEK:

'THE MIGHTY LAND FEATURES WEAPONRY, CLOTHING, FOOTWEAR, JEWELLERY, GEMSTONES, SHIPS, BOATS, RAFTS, MAPS, RIVERS, SEAS, HOT TUBS, COLD POOLS, GARDENS, ORCHARDS, FORESTS, FORTRESSES, FARMS, CASTLES, LIBRARIES, ICE CAVES, CRYSTAL CAVERNS, GLOWING ROCKS, AN IMPOSSIBLY HIGH TOWER, AND A GREAT DEAL OF FOOD.

ALSO, THERE ARE FESTIVALS, BETROTHALS, WEDDINGS, BABIES, FASHION SHOWS, GOOD SONGS, BAD JOKES, SPECTRAL RESONANCE, MUSIC, AUGURY, AND GEOMANCY. THERE ARE ANIMALS TOO: CATS, DOGS, SHEEP, GOATS, MULES, OXEN, BEARS, DOLPHINS, PORPOISES, AND MANY KINDS OF BIRDS. ALSO SOME CREATURES NOT ENCOUNTERED BEFORE; SOME ARE FRIENDLY, OTHERS ARE THREATENING.'

FROM PIPPA AGRIPPA IN BRITANNIA PRIMA:

CHAPTER ONE - APPLE CAKE

PIPPA IN CONVERSATION WITH ERASMUS, HER COMMANDING OFFICER AND MENTOR:

'"EVEN SO, AGRIPPA," HE HAD TOLD HER, "YOU ARE DESTINED TO DO GREAT DEEDS. TO WALK WITH GIANTS. ASK THE AUGUR IF YOU DON'T BELIEVE ME. THE BIRDS DON'T LIE." HE WINKED KNOWINGLY.

SHE WAS SURPRISED. SHE HAD BEEN HERE FOR A YEAR. SHE DIDN'T KNOW THE CAMP HAD AN AUGUR: ONE WHO MAKES PREDICTIONS AND INTERPRETATIONS BASED ON THE BEHAVIOUR OF BIRDS.'

CHAPTER TWO - PUSHING AND PULLING

DURING HER TIME AT VINDAVIA NOVA:

'OCCASIONALLY, SHE WOULD GO TO TRAIN, OR HAVE A CLASS WITH THE ARES MONS... THE DATE WAS SET FOR THE WEDDING OF TERRANES AND JULIA: ON THE FINAL DAY OF MAIA; THE EVE OF THE KALENDS OF JUNO.

DIMOCLETUS HAD EMPLOYED AN AUGUR TO WATCH THE BIRDS IN ORDER TO CHOOSE AN AUSPICIOUS TIME. FOR A BRITANNIC FAMILY WITH NO SECOND NAME, PHILIPPA THOUGHT, THEY ARE MORE ROMAN THAN ANY OF US.'

TREYA MEYNACK IN THE WESTERN AIR

CHAPTER THREE - MUTUAL SUPPORT

TREYA THE SCRIBE IS INTRODUCED TO MASTER OCCUL'S TEXT:

'TREYA WENT TO THE KOVSKRIFVA EARLY, TO GET HER SCRIBING DONE BEFORE THE MEETING. LUGARN WASN'T THERE, BELOW OR ABOVE. MASTER SKELL WAS AT HIS DESK.
SHE SAID, "GOOD DAY, MASTER SKELL," AS USUAL.
"A GOOD DAY TO YOU, TREYA MEYNACK," HE REPLIED.

HE DIDN'T LOOK UP, SO SHE CONTINUED TO HER DESK AND SAT.

THERE WAS A NEW ASSIGNMENT WAITING FOR HER:

ORNITHOMANCY AND AUGURY, AN ILLUSTRATED PRACTICAL HISTORY.

BY OCCUL OF LUGDUNEN, PRAEFECTUS AUGERES

CONTENTS:

BASIC ORNITHOMANCY
AUGURY AND INAUGURATION- AUSPICIOUS AND INAUSPICIOUS OMENS
FEATHERS AND FLIGHT- WING SHAPE, AIRFLOW, GROUP MOVEMENT
TRACKING MOVEMENT PATTERNS- DEXTER, SINISTER, LAGOMORPH, CONVEX, CONCAVE, AND MIRRORED
THE BIRDS EYE VIEW- CASTING THE ATTENTION UPWARD AND GAZING DOWN
TEMPLUMS AND QUADRANTS- USING THE LITUUS TO APPORTION AND EXAMINE THE SKIES
NORTH VERSES SOUTH- A CULTURAL OVERVIEW OF ALIGNMENTS
LEFT TO RIGHT- UTILISING INSTINCT TO GUIDE REASON
RIGHT TO LEFT- EMPLOYING REASON TO TEMPER INSTINCT

THE LANGUAGES OF BIRDS
THE CALLS OF THE SEA BIRDS- GULLS, PLOVERS, PIPERS AND TERNS
THE CALLS OF THE SINGING BIRDS- LARKS, NIGHTINGALES AND MOORHENS
THE CALLS OF THE SMALL BIRDS- SPARROWS, WRENS, ROBINS, AND BLACKBIRDS
THE CALLS OF THE RAPTORS- HAWKS, KITES, AND FALCONS

THE CALLS OF THE UNEARTHLY BIRDS- OWLS, CUCKOO, FLAGEOLETS, AND MOCKINGBIRDS
THE CALLS OF THE GROWLING BIRDS- JAYS, JACKDAWS, MAGPIES, CROWS, AND RAVENS
THE EXALTED REALM OF THE DEATH EATERS- BUZZARDS AND VULTURES
THE SUPREME RULERS OF THE SKY- EAGLES AND THEIR PORTENTS
THE BIRDS AND THE COSMOS- THE PLANETS, MOON, SUN, AND STARS, AND THE LATITUDINAL SHIFT OF THE SKIES
WHAT BIRDS SEE AND HEAR- BEYOND THE HUMAN SPECTRA OF LIGHT AND SOUND

PRINCIPLES OF AUGURY

AUGURY: MAGICAL DIVINATION, OR MERE NATURAL OBSERVATION?
RECOGNISING PATTERNS- SEASONAL, ANNUAL, AND EPOCHAL
MESSAGES FROM THE GODS- BLESSINGS, PROPHECIES AND WARNINGS
'SORT SOL' - THE BLACK SUN, GOOD OR BAD OMEN?
AUGURIES OF THE FUTURE- PORTENTS, DIVINATIONS AND PETITIONS
WEARING THE HOOD- PROTOCOLS FOR INTERACTING WITH OFFICIALS, AND WITH THE PUBLIC

Treya found herself reading the document. It seemed like a good opportunity to learn to identify the winged creatures of the surface world. It was interesting, too, especially the parts about the bird's eye view. There were eighteen pages of densely packed text and images. She began copying the text, leaving spaces for the pictures, which she would put in afterwards. She didn't really care for rendering images, but she often found herself doing it anyway.'

'When the noon bell rang in the distance, she cleaned her pen and straightened her area. She rose, took the step ladder from its corner, and set it in front of the shelf. The food box was the only thing that the stepladder was used for, yet the step ladder had to be stored in the far corner.

It was all a bit of a nuisance. It made sense to have a food box, but why it had to be so high up, or why it wasn't kept in the small alcove, where the eating actually took place, she didn't understand.

Treya opened the box. She was pleased to see that the fellows had been enjoying the plum cakes she had brought. She took one out, along with a chunk of yellow cheese, and wrapped them in a cloth. She closed the box and climbed back down.

Holding the bundle carefully in one hand, she moved the stepladder back to its spot. Then she slipped into the little alcove. She set her food on the table, washed and dried her hands, and poured a drink of water.

As she ate, she stared out of the narrow window. Seabirds were flying around over the harbor. She thought of what she'd learned about the way that birds moved: dexter, sinister, lagomorph, concave, convex, and mirrored- that meant right, left,

MOVING SHAPE, CURVED DOWN, CURVED UP, AND SYMMETRICAL. SHE WATCHED THE BIRDS.

SHE RECOGNISED THE GULLS, RAZORBILLS AND TERNS FROM THEIR PICTURES. THEY WERE HUNTING FOR FISH, SWOOPING AND DIVING IN AND OUT OF VIEW. THEIR MOVEMENTS WERE ERRATIC. IT WASN'T MUCH FOR AN ORNITHOMANCER TO WORK WITH.

STILL, SHE ASKED HERSELF, WHAT CAN BE LEARNED FROM WATCHING THEM? WELL, SHE THOUGHT, IF BIRDS ARE CATCHING FISH, THAT WOULD TELL THE FISHERMEN WHERE TO CAST THEIR NETS. IT SEEMED QUITE OBVIOUS, BUT IT WAS STILL AN EXAMPLE OF BASIC ORNITHOMANCY.

THE NEXT DAY, PHILIPPA JOINS TREYA IN STUDYING THE TEXT:

"COME AND SEE," SAID TREYA. SHE AND PIPPA WENT OVER TO TREYA'S DESK.

"I'M WORKING ON SOMETHING FUN FOR A CHANGE," SHE SAID, SHOWING PIPPA THE NEW MANUSCRIPT. "IT'S ABOUT THE AUGURY OF BIRDS. I WAS THINKING THAT YOU MIGHT BE INTERESTED IN THAT."

"I AM INTERESTED IN THAT," PIPPA REPLIED. THEY BOTH SAT. PIPPA EXAMINED THE DOCUMENT.

"I'VE HEARD ABOUT THE AUGURS," SHE SAID. 'BEFORE I LEFT ARES MONS TRAINING CAMP, MY CENTURION, ARIES ERASMUS, CLAIMED THE BIRDS HAD PREDICTED THAT I WOULD DO GREAT THINGS... THAT I WOULD WALK WITH GIANTS." SHE GREW SILENT, MOMENTARILY LOST IN THOUGHT. "I SUPPOSE THEY WERE RIGHT. EVEN THOUGH

THAT'S PROBABLY WHAT WAS SAID TO EVERY NEW SOLDIER AS THEY STARTED THEIR CAREER."

PIPPA BEGAN READING THE CONTENTS PAGE.

"THIS IS REALLY GOOD," SHE SAID. "WE SHOULD HAVE A COPY FOR OURSELVES."
"I'D LIKE THAT," SAID TREYA. "I'M NOT USUALLY INTERESTED IN WHAT I'M SCRIBING, BUT THIS IS DIFFERENT."
"MASTER SKELL," PIPPA SAID, TURNING AROUND. "IS IT ALRIGHT IF WE COPY THIS FOR OURSELVES TOO?"

"OF COURSE, COUNCILOR," HE REPLIED.

"PIPPA, WOULD YOU BE WILLING TO DRAW THE PICTURES ON BOTH COPIES?" ASKED TREYA. "I CAN FLY THROUGH THE TEXT, BUT THE IMAGES REALLY SLOW ME DOWN."

"THAT SOUNDS LIKE A PERFECT ARRANGEMENT," SAID PIPPA. "YOU FLY THROUGH THE TEXT AND I'LL FLY THROUGH THE PICTURES."

"WE'LL FLY," SAID TREYA, "LIKE THE BIRDS.'"

....

LATER:

'THEY TOOK THEIR SEATS AND FOUND THEIR PLACES. THEY WERE ON THE CHAPTER TITLED 'TEMPLUMS AND QUADRANTS- USING THE LITUUS TO APPORTION AND EXAMINE THE SKIES'. THERE WERE SEVERAL PICTURES OF THE LITUUS, WHICH WAS A STICK THAT TERMINATED IN A GRACEFUL LOOP.

"IT'S PRETTY," SAID PIPPA. "HOW DOES IT WORK?"

TREYA READ OUT LOUD:

"THE LITUUS IS THE AUGUR'S WAND. IT IS A STAFF WITH A SPIRAL CROOK, USED TO DIVIDE THE SKY INTO QUADRANTS AND MARK OUT THE TEMPLUM, A RITUAL SPACE IN THE AIR. THE PASSAGE OF BIRDS THROUGH THIS TEMPLUM INDICATES DIVINE FAVOUR OR DISFAVOUR FOR A GIVEN UNDERTAKING. THE LITUUS IS ALSO USED AS A SYMBOL OF OFFICE FOR THE COLLEGE OF THE AUGURS TO MARK THEM OUT AS A PRIESTLY GROUP."

"IT'S A NICE SHAPE," SAID PIPPA. "IT LOOKS LIKE THE HEAD FEATHER OF ONE OF KING ARAWN'S FANCY GROUND-BIRDS."

TREYA CONTINUED:

"THE LITUUS SPIRAL IS A MANIFESTATION OF THE GOLDEN MEAN. IT IS A TWO-DIMENSIONAL POLAR COORDINATE

SYSTEM, A SPIRAL IN WHICH THE VARIABLE OF THE ANGLE IS... INVERSELY PROPORTIONAL TO THE SQUARE OF THE RADIUS."

THE TWO WOMEN LOOKED AT EACH OTHER AND SPONTANEOUSLY BURST INTO GIGGLES.

"DID YOU UNDERSTAND THAT?" ASKED TREYA.

"NOT AT ALL!" PIPPA LAUGHED. "BUT IT SOUNDS IMPRESSIVE. I LIKE THE LITUUS. IF WE'RE TO BE AUGERS WE'LL EACH NEED ONE."

"PERHAPS THE SMITHS COULD MAKE THEM," TREYA SUGGESTED.

"I WAS JUST THINKING THAT VERY THING," PIPPA REPLIED, SMILING.'

CHAPTER FIVE - AUSPICIOUS PORTENTS

TREYA AND PIPPA PERFORM AN AUGURY ON THE HILLSIDE OVERLOOKING THE SOUTH HARBOUR OF TINTAGEL, IN ADVANCE OF THEIR UPCOMING SEA JOURNEY:

'THEY WERE WEARING THE HOODED AUGUR CLOAKS THAT LOWI HAD MADE FOR THEM, WHICH WERE CREAM-COLOURED WITH PURPLE BORDERS. THEY EACH CARRIED AN ELEGANT LITUUS. TREYA'S WAS MADE OF WILLOW, TRAINED INTO A SPIRAL AND ATTACHED TO A CAST BRONZE HANDLE. PIPPA'S SPIRAL WAS OF CARVED CEDAR, ON A HANDLE OF FINELY WROUGHT TIN.

TREYA WAS HAVING TROUBLE FOCUSING. SHE WAS THINKING ABOUT THE UPCOMING SHIP JOURNEY. SHE WAS DREADING A REPEAT OF HER PREVIOUS ILLNESS.

PIPPA HAD ASSURED HER THAT SHE WOULD DO MUCH BETTER THIS TIME, BEING MORE ACCUSTOMED TO THE SURFACE WORLD.

LOWI, WHO WAS GOING TOO, WAS BRINGING TINCTURES OF MINT AND CHAMOMILE, TO SOOTH ANY SEA-SICKNESS. STILL, ARGHAN REMINDED THEM, AS THE SEA CHURNS, SO DOES THE GUT, AND THERE'S NOTHING ANYONE CAN DO ABOUT IT. TREYA WAS RELIEVED THAT IT APPEARED TO BE A SHORT SEA JOURNEY TO DINAS DINLLE.

TREYA AND PIPPA WERE PERFORMING THIS AUGURY IN ADVANCE OF THEIR UPCOMING JOURNEY. PIPPA STOOD FACING THE SEA, AND THE OPEN HORIZON. TREYA FACED THE HILLS, AND THE CLIFFS THAT BORDERED THE WEST SIDE OF TREVENA CASTLE.

SHE HAD NEVER BEEN TO THE WESTERN HARBOUR BEFORE. SHE LOOKED UP AT THE WALLS OF THE CASTLE. IT WAS FROM ONE OF THOSE HIGH TERRACES THAT THEY HAD THROWN MIMI RYEA'S CLOTHING. THAT WHOLE INCIDENT SEEMED LIKE A DREAM, ALMOST AS THOUGH IT HAD HAPPENED TO SOMEONE ELSE.

STARING AT THE SKY NOW, SHE WAS FEELING NERVOUS. SHE REMEMBERED HER AN DHEW TRAINING, AND STEADIED HER BREATH. SHE AND PIPPA STOOD IN SILENCE, BACK TO BACK, HOODS UP, EACH PEERING INTO THEIR OWN TEMPLUM IN THE SKY THAT THEY HAD MAPPED OUT WITH THEIR SPIRAL WANDS.

ACCORDING TO OCCUL OF LUGDUNEN, THERE WERE CONFLICTING CULTURAL VIEWS OVER WHETHER AN AUGUR SHOULD FACE NORTH OR SOUTH, SO THEY HAD DECIDED THAT SINCE THEY WERE A TEAM, THEY WOULD DO BOTH, AND COMPARE THEIR FINDINGS.

TREYA DREW A LONG SLOW BREATH AND FOCUSED HER ATTENTION. SHE COULD HEAR DISTANT GULLS, CRYING LOUDLY ALL OF A SUDDEN, BUT NO BIRDS HAD APPEARED IN HER QUADRANT. AS SHE GAZED, HER MIND WANDERED BACK TO THE TIME SHE HAD SPENT ON THE PEAKS OVER THE RED SANDS. SHE RECALLED THE HAZY CEILING OF THE CAVERN, AND THE BIRDS THAT WHEELED AROUND NEAR THE SKY-CRACKS.

COMPARED TO THE PALE FISH-CATCHERS THAT POPULATED THE UNDERGROUND WORLD, THEY HAD LOOKED VERY LARGE. AT THE TIME, WITH THEIR SILVER-GREY PLUMAGE AND SHINY GREEN HEADS, THEY HAD SEEMED EXOTIC TO HER.

NOW SHE REALISED THAT THEY WERE COMMON DOVES. SHE STILL THOUGHT THAT THEY WERE BEAUTIFUL, BUT SHE UNDERSTOOD THAT THEY WERE NOT CONSIDERED VERY EXOTIC AT ALL BY MOST SURFACE-DWELLERS.

THE CRIES OF THE GULLS BECAME MORE INSISTENT. THEN TREYA REALISED WHY. A WHITE-TAILED SEA-EAGLE HAD APPEARED IN HER TEMPLUM, FLYING DIAGONALLY FROM LOWER LEFT TO UPPER RIGHT.

AN EAGLE! TREYA THOUGHT. THE MOST AUSPICIOUS OF ALL THE BIRDS, FLYING LEFT TO RIGHT. BEGINNING IN THE REALM OF INSTINCT, AND BECOMING RARIFIED THROUGH REASON.

THEN ANOTHER SEA-EAGLE APPEARED! IT CAME FROM THE LOWER RIGHT, AND FLEW TOWARDS THE UPPER LEFT.

RIGHT TO LEFT: REASON IS LIMITED UNTIL IT EMBRACES INSTINCT.

THEN THEY WERE GONE FROM VIEW.

PIPPA EXCLAIMED, "WHAT GLORIOUS EAGLES!"

THEN TREYA REALISED THAT THE TWO BIRDS WERE FLYING AROUND BOTH OF THE AUGERS.

THEY SOON REAPPEARED IN TREYA'S TEMPLUM.

PRACTITIONERS OF AUGURY WERE MEANT TO WITHHOLD DIVINATION UNTIL AFTER THE OBSERVATIONS WERE COMPLETE, BUT TREYA COULDN'T HELP THINKING THAT SEA-EAGLES ASCENDING IN A SPIRAL PATTERN WAS AN AUSPICIOUS SIGN FOR A JOURNEY BY SHIP TO FIND A SPIRAL CASTLE.

THE TEMPLUM WAS EMPTY AGAIN. TREYA CLOSED IT WITH HER LITUUS. BEHIND HER, SHE COULD FEEL PIPPA CLOSING HERS TOO.

THEY TURNED TO FACE EACH OTHER. THEN THEY BOTH LOOKED UP, THEIR HOODS DROPPING BEHIND THEM.

THE TWO EAGLES WERE STILL CIRCLING, CLIMBING HIGHER AND HIGHER, UNTIL FINALLY THEY BECAME LITTLE SPECKS AND DISAPPEARED FROM VIEW. THE TWO FRIENDS GRINNED AT EACH OTHER. THEN THEY WENT TO FIND THEIR COMPANIONS, TO TELL THEM OF THE AUSPICIOUS PORTENTS.'

CHAPTER SEVEN STRENGTH IN SILLINESS

BEFORE LEAVING SHOE ISLE:

'THEY SET OUT THE NEXT DAY. TREYA AND PIPPA HAD GOTTEN UP EARLY TO VIEW THE BIRDS FROM THE BOW OF THE MORHOGH. ARGHAN, MASTER SKELL, AND LOWI HAD WATCHED WITH THEM. AS THEY HELD UP THEIR AUGURY WANDS, THE FIRST RAYS OF THE SUN WERE JUST BEGINNING TO PIERCE THROUGH THE MORNING MIST.

THEY HEARD THE BIRDS BEFORE THEY CAME INTO VIEW. A HAWK WAS BEING CONFRONTED BY TWO RAVENS. THE RAVENS WOULD DIVE AT THE HAWK, THEN THE HAWK WOULD QUICKLY THREATEN THE RAVENS, ONE AT A TIME.

THERE WAS A GREAT DEAL OF LOUD SQUAWKING. EVENTUALLY THE HAWK FLEW AWAY TO THE NORTH AND THE RAVENS TO THE EAST.

"WHAT DO YOU SUPPOSE IT MEANS?" ASKED TREYA, CLOSING HER TEMPLUM. SHE PULLED DOWN HER HOOD.

"WELL," PIPPA REPLIED, DOING THE SAME. "THEY HAD A CONFLICT. IT SEEMED LIKE THINGS WOULD GET VIOLENT, BUT THEY NEVER DID. THEN THEY WENT THEIR SEPARATE WAYS. IS THERE SOMETHING TO CONCLUDE FROM THAT?"

THE WOMEN WERE SILENT, STARING AT THE PEACEFUL SKY.

"MAYBE," SAID ARGHAN, "IT MEANS THAT IF WE RUN INTO TROUBLE, WE NEED TO NOT LET IT ESCALATE INTO VIOLENCE. WE SHOULD TEMPER INSTINCT WITH REASON, LIKE YOUR BIRD-BOOK SAYS."

"THAT SOUNDS LIKE GOOD ADVICE," SAID MASTER SKELL.'

THE SHIP APPROACHES A BEACH ON THE WAY TO THULE

"'TREAFADDYRD!"

PIRI CRIED FROM THE LOOKOUT. PIRAN CLIMBED QUICKLY UP TO THE WATCH PLATFORM. PIRI CAME DOWN AND JOINED THE COMPANIONS. THE SHIP ENTERED A SMALL SECLUDED BAY. THE WATER WAS TURQUOISE BLUE AND AMAZINGLY CLEAR. IT WAS INDEED FULL OF ROCKS. THEY WERE DARK RED AND BLACK, WITH BANDS OF ORANGE AND PALE GREEN. SOME WERE BIG, LIKE ISLANDS, AND COVERED WITH LICHEN AND SEAWEED. OTHERS WERE HIDDEN JUST BELOW THE WATER.

THE SHIP MOVED CAUTIOUSLY AROUND THE OBSTACLES.

ON ONE OF THE ISLANDS, A FLOCK OF CORMORANTS WERE SUNNING THEIR WIDE-OPEN WINGS.

"CORMORANTS," SAID PIPPA. SHE COUNTED QUICKLY. "SEVEN OF THEM."

"WHAT SAY YOU, AUGERS?" MASTER SKELL ASKED. "WHAT SORT OF OMEN IS IT?"

LOWI SUDDENLY WENT BELOW DECK.

"AUGERS!" SAID MARCUS. "WHAT DO YOU MEAN, SIR?"

"THE LADIES ARE REVIVING THE ANCIENT PRACTICE OF PREDICTIVE ORNITHOMANCY."

"TELLING THE FUTURE WITH BIRDS?" HE ASKED INCREDULOUSLY.

"IT'S MORE OF A PROCESS OF REFLECTING ON OBSERVATIONS OF THE NATURAL WORLD," SAID PIPPA.

LOWI RETURNED. SHE HANDED EACH AUGUR THEIR LITUUS AND DRAPED THEM WITH THEIR ROBES. TREYA AND PIPPA PULLED UP THEIR HOODS AND STOOD BACK TO BACK.

THEY EACH RAISED THEIR TEMPLUM AND WAITED. TREYA STARED. UNLIKE ON LAND, THE SCENE CHANGED AS THE BOAT DRIFTED ALONG.

THE CORMORANTS RECEDED, AND FIVE SLEEK- LOOKING DUCKS CAME INTO VIEW. THEY HAD BLUE AND WHITE BODIES AND SHINY GREEN HEADS. THEY WERE RELAXING ON THE ROCKS. THE LARGEST MALE QUACKED LOUDLY AS THE SHIP CRAWLED PAST.

TREYA FELT PIPPA CLOSING HER TEMPLUM, SO SHE DID TOO.

SHE LOWERED HER HOOD AND THEY BOTH TURNED TOWARD THE OTHERS.

"WHATEVER YOU'RE UP TO, AUGERS," SAID BRUTUS, "IT CERTAINLY LOOKS IMPRESSIVE."

"WELL," SAID TREYA, "ASIDE FROM THE SEVEN CORMORANTS DRYING THEIR WINGS, I'VE GOT FIVE COLOURFUL DUCKS, RESTING ON AN ISLAND. THE DRAKE WAS QUITE VIGILANT."

"I'VE GOT THREE BUZZARDS, GLIDING ON THE AIR," SAID PIPPA.

"SO?" SAID MARCUS. "WHAT DOES IT MEAN?"

"I DON'T KNOW," SAID TREYA. "PIPPA?"

"HMMM," PIPPA SAID. "RIGHT THEN. THE SEVEN CORMORANTS DRYING THEIR WINGS, THAT'S US, THE SEVEN PASSENGERS WHO CAME FROM TREVENA. WE'RE POWERFUL, BUT SOMETIMES WE'RE VULNERABLE, LIKE THEM."

"FROM THEM WE LEARN THAT THERE IS TIME FOR ACTION AND A TIME TO BE STILL. AND LIKE THEM, WE DRAW STRENGTH FROM THE LIGHT, AND IT PROTECTS US."

"THE FIVE DUCKS ARE OUR FRIENDS FROM THE SOUTH. THEY'RE GROUNDED AND CONFIDENT, FULL OF KNOWLEDGE AND GIFTS TO SHARE. AND THEY'RE VERY ATTRACTIVE."

"SO ATTRACTIVE, THAT STRANGERS MAY SOMETIMES BE A LITTLE TOO INTERESTED, SO THEY MUST REMAIN VIGILANT, BUT RELAXED."

"THE THREE BUZZARDS ARE THE CREW OF THE MORHOGH-"

"WE'RE BUZZARDS?" EXCLAIMED PIRI INDIGNANTLY.

"THE BUZZARD IS HIGHLY RESPECTED IN MANY CULTURES," SAID MASTER SKELL, "AND RANKS HIGH IN THE ORNITHOLOGICAL HIERARCHY."

"THEY RIDE THE WIND," SAID PIPPA. "THEY KNOW THE WIND. THEY ARE SKILLED NAVIGATORS, AND MASTERS OF ANY SITUATION. WE TRUST THEM TO KNOW WHAT TO DO."

"OH, THAT'S ALRIGHT THEN," SAID PIRI, GRINNING.

"WELL DONE, AUGERS," SAID LORD GWYDION.'

ND - #0157 - 080726 - C0 - 229/152/5 - PB - 9798992037661 - Gloss Lamination